The Essential Guide

Written by Barbara Bazaldua

CONTENTS

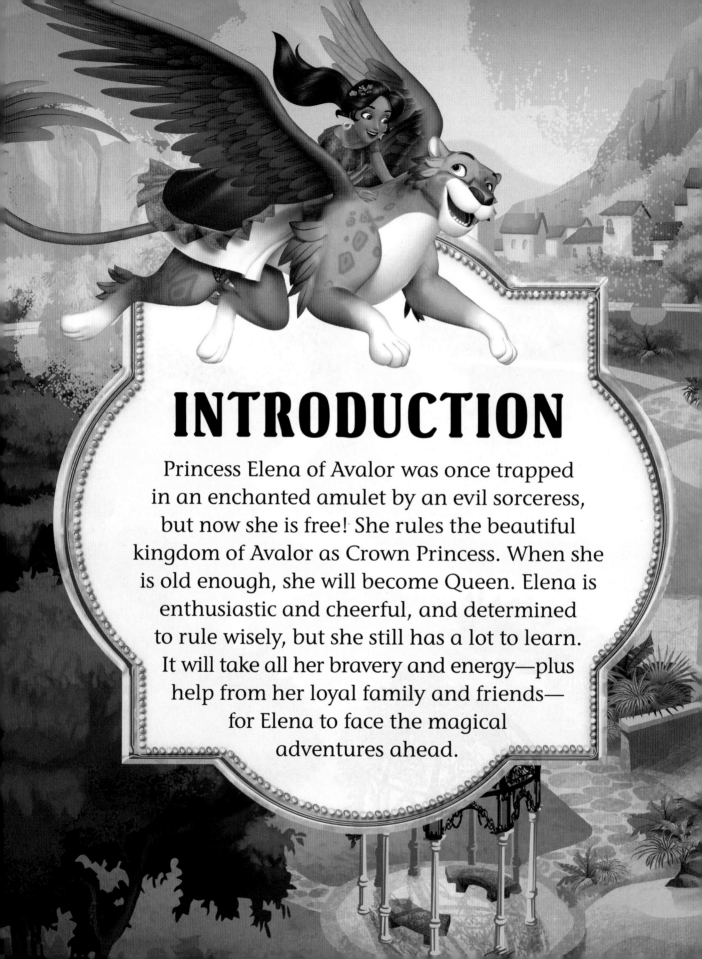

INTRODUCTION

Princess Elena of Avalor was once trapped
in an enchanted amulet by an evil sorceress,
but now she is free! She rules the beautiful
kingdom of Avalor as Crown Princess. When she
is old enough, she will become Queen. Elena is
enthusiastic and cheerful, and determined
to rule wisely, but she still has a lot to learn.
It will take all her bravery and energy—plus
help from her loyal family and friends—
for Elena to face the magical
adventures ahead.

ELENA

As Crown Princess of Avalor, 16-year-old Elena has a lot of responsibility on her shoulders. Luckily, she is smart, brave, and full of energy! Best of all, she can laugh and learn from her mistakes.

Fresh Avaloran flowers

Maruvian gold jewelry

Side by side

Elena knows she can achieve anything with family and friends by her side. She can be overprotective of her sister Isabel, but that's what big sisters are for!

Red is bright and strong, just like Elena.

Brave of heart

Elena has the courage to listen to others before she judges them. Her understanding often turns creatures who seem scary into friends.

Crown Princess

Crown Princess Elena wants to rule Avalor wisely and well, but she still has a lot to learn before she turns 20 and becomes Queen.

Shoes are perfect for dancing.

> *"I vow to protect and defend the kingdom of Avalor."* Elena

Have you heard?

Elena's time in the magical amulet has given her some magical powers.

Spirited chats

One of Elena's magic abilities allows her to see animal spirit guides. Zuzo, a spirit fox, often offers Elena his special spirit wisdom.

True or false?

Elena was trapped inside a magical amulet for 10 years!

False.
She was imprisoned in it for 41 years.

Scepter power

Controlling her magical Scepter is tricky, but Elena is a fast learner. She masters some of the Scepter's powers when she uses it to defeat Orizaba, the moth fairy.

7

ROYAL PALACE

The elegant Royal Palace has been the official residence for the rulers of the kingdom of Avalor for many centuries. Now it is home sweet home for Crown Princess Elena and her family.

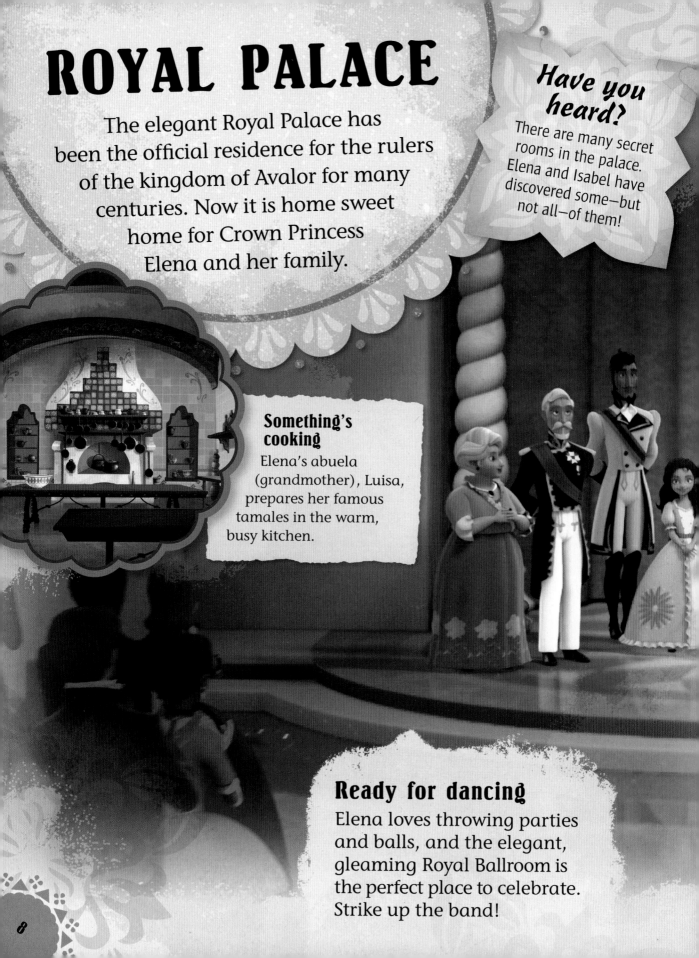

Have you heard?

There are many secret rooms in the palace. Elena and Isabel have discovered some—but not all—of them!

Something's cooking

Elena's abuela (grandmother), Luisa, prepares her famous tamales in the warm, busy kitchen.

Ready for dancing

Elena loves throwing parties and balls, and the elegant, gleaming Royal Ballroom is the perfect place to celebrate. Strike up the band!

Dream room
Elena's brightly colored bedroom has everything she needs for relaxing. Sweet dreams, Princess!

Throne decorated with traditional Avaloran designs.

Columns made of solid Maruvian gold.

Polished floor is perfect for gliding and waltzing.

Beautiful setting
The Royal Palace is built into towering cliffs above a sparkling waterfall. A graceful bridge leads to the town of Avalor.

The Avalor Times

PALACE LIFE
A BEHIND-THE-SCENES LOOK

Crown Princess Elena is devoting herself to an increasing number of royal duties, which keep her busy from breakfast until bedtime. Our roving reporter takes a look at some of the Princess's most important tasks, with exclusive insights from her loyal head courtier, Armando.

Armando, Chief of Staff, Royal Palace

"Princess Elena is caring, confident, and great to work with. She is very busy, but always makes time for me."

ARMANDO

As Chief of Staff, Armando has his hands full of things for Elena to sign, such as this proclamation about an upcoming Royal Visit.

KEEPING THE CITY RUNNING

Elena meets with harbormaster Captain Turner to ask for his ideas to make Avalor an even better place to live.

BRAND NEW BRIDGE!

Plans are under way for a bridge connecting Avalor and the kingdom of Cordoba. This is Crown Princess Elena's first big royal project and she's thrilled.

ROYALS VISIT AVALOR

> **"Elena's first Royal Visit from King Toshi of Satu was a huge success after they discovered the importance of family in both cultures."**
>
> ARMANDO

Princess Elena welcomes King Toshi before introducing him to her family. King Toshi is eager to learn about the kingdom of Avalor.

COUNCIL MEETINGS NOW HELD DAILY

It has been announced that the new Grand Council appointed by Crown Princess Elena will meet every morning. The Council will discuss everything from palace events to the dangers that may threaten Avalor. Avaloran citizens will be able to address the Council directly, if they wish.

LUISA AND FRANCISCO

Elena's grandparents want to help her be the best ruler she can be! Francisco sticks to tradition, while Luisa is open to new ideas. Elena relies on both of them for advice.

Proud abuelo

Francisco can be stubborn about doing things his way, but he is always happy when Elena makes a great choice on her own.

Singing sensation

Francisco often uses music to teach a lesson, tell a story, or just to celebrate. His songs are a high note at every occasion.

Traditional royal uniform

Wise, patient expression

True or false?

Francisco and Luisa's last name is Flores.

True. It means "flowers".

Made with love

Luisa is an excellent cook and she enjoys cooking traditional food for her family. It's a delicious way to show her love.

Wiser advisors

Elena is so energetic that she can be a bit impulsive. Her grandparents gently remind her to slow down and look before she leaps. It is wise advice.

"There's always a bright side!"
Luisa to Elena

Smart abuela

Luisa is a good listener and observer. She often convinces Francisco to see things from another point of view.

Loving smile

Necklace of blue jewels

Have you heard?

Luisa and Francisco come from a long line of Avaloran nobility. They are the parents of Elena's mom, Queen Lucia.

13

MUSIC IS MAGIC

The people of Avalor love music, especially Elena, who is a wonderful guitarist and singer. Whatever the situation, there is always a heartfelt song to help anyone who needs it.

"I'm ready to rule now!" **Elena to Francisco**

Musical debate
Elena thinks she is ready to be Queen. Francisco doesn't agree. When they sing about their different opinions, they find a harmony between them.

"You're still learning. So am I." **Elena to Mateo**

A song of encouragement
Mateo doubts his wizarding skills, but Elena sings him an encouraging song. Listening to Elena's music, Mateo's confidence is boosted.

"You're already someone special to me." **Captain Turner to Naomi**

Special hopes

When Naomi is asked to lead an archaeological dig, she sings about her wish to show people that she's someone special.

"I'll always have time for you!" **Elena to Isabel**

Sisterly love

When Isabel feels sad because she thinks Elena can't spend time with her, Elena cheers her up with an upbeat tune about spending lots of sister time together!

ISABEL

Elena's adoring 10-year-old sister, Isabel, is a brilliant, budding inventor. She loves science, math, and solving problems. Isabel is eager to try anything and go anywhere—especially if it means making new discoveries.

Curious mind

Isabel wants to know about everything. However, her curiosity sometimes leads her and others into trouble!

True or false?

Isabel has magical powers, just like her big sister, Elena.

False. Isabel is super smart, but she has no magical abilities.

Sister team

While Isabel looks up to her confident big sister, Elena sometimes relies on Isabel to come up with solutions to tricky problems.

"There's so much stuff I wanna do!" **Isabel**

Busy, busy brain

Isabel's mind is always working. Give her some tools and a problem to solve, and she's happy.

Prized possession

Isabel's journal is precious to her. It's jammed with calculations, drawings, and ideas.

Never leaves home without her journal.

Have you heard?

Isabel was trapped in an enchanted painting for 41 years, or as she calculates it, 14,965 days!

Short skirt makes exploring easier.

Proud to be different

Because she's so smart, Isabel often feels different than other kids. Luckily Elena is always there to tell her to be proud of who she is.

ISABEL'S INVENTIONS

It seems as if Isabel dreams up a new invention every day! Where does she get her amazing ideas? From her imagination, of course.

Made of an umbrella, rope, and glass jar.

Magnophone

Imagine being able to hear sounds from miles away! Isabel is excited—maybe the Magnophone will help her hear Marposas whistling.

Looks like an ordinary wooden wardrobe.

Powered by pedaling.

Presto Changer

The Presto Changer is such a helpful invention. It puts your clothes on for you—and even matches socks perfectly! What a great time-saver!

Guitardion

Isabel's latest musical invention combines two instruments. Playing the Guitardion is like being a one-princess band.

Guitar + accordion = fun sounds.

Made from a telescope.

Solar projector

Safety first! Isabel's clever solar projector shows an image of the sun on a wall, so everyone can watch the solar eclipse without hurting their eyes.

Never give up

When Isabel's inventions don't work the first time round, she tinkers, tests, and tries, tries again.

MATEO

Mateo is Avalor's youngest and least experienced Royal Wizard ever! Luckily, he is smart and a fast learner. Mateo often makes jokes to hide his sensitive feelings. But he is always serious about helping his friends.

Tamborita helps with spells.

Simple clothing allows freedom of movement.

Learning to spell

To cast a spell, Mateo strikes his tamborita (drum wand) and says the magic words. He is getting better every day!

True or false?

Mateo's spirit guide is an armadillo.

False. It's a blue three-toed sloth called a cacahuate.

Growing confidence

Mateo sometimes doubts his magical skills, but he has what it takes to become a great wizard. Elena is always around to encourage him.

"I am honored to serve the kingdom." **Mateo**

Ancient wisdom

When Mateo finds his grandfather's ancient spellbook, he discovers a treasure trove of magic.

Royal robes

In honor of Mateo's new role as Royal Wizard, Elena gives him the robes his grandfather once wore.

Have you heard?

Magic runs in Mateo's family. His grandfather, Alacazar, was also a Royal Wizard.

Potions master

Making potions can be tricky. Mateo rises to the challenge when he prepares one to undo a spell cast by the wicked wizard Fiero.

Duendes

These little green elves are up to no good! They want to bring thousands more rascally duendes into Avalor. Elena quickly realizes that they must be stopped.

Body made of volcanic rock.

MAGICAL CREATURES

As the ruler of Avalor, Elena comes across many magical creatures. She works hard to find out what each creature wants—and does her best to help them, if she can!

Marposas

Marposas are gentle, purple sea creatures. They lay their eggs on the beach. When the babies hatch, they slide into the sea to be with their moms.

Noblins

Noblins are masters of transformation. The purple, fuzzy, goblin-like creatures can turn themselves into dogs, and change objects into gold.

Flames shoot
from head
when angry.

Colorful
rocks are
precious to
Charoca.

Charoca

This gigantic, man-shaped pile
of rock sets off a volcano when
he is angry. Charoca tries to
stay calm, but it's hard when
people steal his beloved rocks.

ZUZO THE SPIRIT FOX

Zuzo, a glowing blue fox, is Elena's personal spirit guide (chanul). He guides Elena through her magical adventures and helps her communicate with the spirit world.

"I'll be back in two shakes of a spirit's tail!"

"Trust me. I know a few things!"

"Are you ready to learn? 'Cause that's all that matters."

Patient teacher

Zuzo is always willing to share his knowledge with Elena. How she uses it is up to her.

Wise fox

Zuzo often teases Elena, but he's very wise. He's been around for centuries and knows a lot. He also knows that Elena must figure out some things on her own.

"Zuzo is on the job. Now tell me exactly what you know."

Mysterious Scepter

Even Zuzo doesn't know what Elena needs to do to control her Scepter. He will do everything he can to find out, though!

"Giving advice is easy. Taking it is the hard part."

"This is the one day a year ghosts come to party with the living."

Party animal

Spirits like Zuzo love the Day of the Dead as much as living humans. The parties are awesome!

AVALOR CITY

Avalor City sits at the heart of the enchanted kingdom of Avalor. With its beautiful Royal Palace, shady plazas, and sunny streets, the city has a special magic of its own. The loyal, happy people of Avalor are proud to call it home.

Have you heard?

Avalor City is built upon the ruins of an ancient civilization known as Maru.

Bright flowers hang over the wall and arch.

The plaza is a popular gathering place.

Chocolate fame

Avalor is renowned for its delicious chocolate. Elena often presents it as a gift during Royal Visits.

Roof terraces are perfect for parties.

Bustling bazaar

The citizens of Avalor shop in the huge, open-air Grand Marketplace. It is a noisy, busy place full of exciting market stalls.

Center for trade

Merchants from all the surrounding kingdoms sail to Avalor for business. It is the busiest port in the world!

Red-tiled rooftops gleam in the sun.

Lively Avalor

Nestled between a sparkling harbor, towering mountains, and deep jungles, Avalor City is full of life. The scents of delicious food, bursts of uplifting music, and happy laughter fill its streets.

ANCIENT LEGENDS

There are many legends in Avalor and its surrounding kingdoms. Most people believe they are just fairy tales, but Elena discovers that many of these stories have a surprising way of coming true!

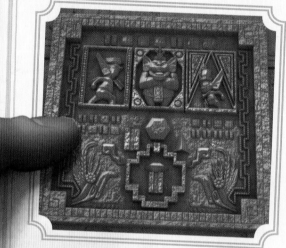

An ancient bronze carving warns of the duende danger.

Duende brothers

Legend tells of three duende brothers who once caused trouble in Avalor, until a wizard locked them up. If they ever break free, they will unlock a tunnel to the duende world, allowing thousands of mischievous duendes to enter Avalor.

The small, green duendes have the power to unlock a gateway into the duende world.

The Yacalli

The people of Cordoba tell of the Yacalli giant, who awakens when his land is dug up or disturbed. The huge wooden creature is strong and looks scary, but he is actually very polite. He even apologizes before causing trouble!

The Yacalli just wants to protect his land and the owls who live there.

Orizaba, the moth fairy

Long ago, this shadowy evil-doer tried to bring eternal darkness to Avalor and was banished to the spirit world by a wizard. But she can return during a solar eclipse, when she will try to work her dark spell on the kingdom once more.

Eye of Midnight
Orizaba searches for the powerful Eye of Midnight, a jewel that can unleash the powers of darkness.

Orizaba prefers darkness to light, and will do all she can to make it dark forever!

NAOMI

Fun-loving, friendly Naomi has a down-to-earth sense of humor and a practical approach to solving problems. It's no wonder Elena likes the outgoing young girl from town the moment they meet.

Harbormaster's daughter

Naomi's father, Captain Turner, is the harbormaster of Avalor. Naomi often helps him at the docks, where she meets many interesting people.

Have you heard?

Naomi's mom is a ship's captain. Recently she was away from home for six months, three weeks, and two days.

On the Grand Council

Elena asks Naomi to join the Grand Council because she knows Naomi has much knowledge to offer. Naomi is honored, but also very nervous.

Freckles from lots of time in the sun.

Someone special

Sometimes, Naomi thinks she must prove that she's not just an ordinary girl. However, her family and friends remind her that they know how special she is!

Always wears her jade bracelet.

Taking responsibility

Naomi is thrilled when Elena appoints her to lead an archaeological dig in Avalor City.

Comfortable boots and clothes for being active

Best friends

Best friends help each other, and Elena and Naomi know they can always count on one another.

31

> ## "We make a pretty good team!"
> ### Naomi to Elena

Fake Princess

During King Toshi's visit, Elena talks Naomi into switching places with her at the palace. Naomi doesn't think she can fake being a Princess, but she gives it a try!

In it together

Naomi and Elena stick together, even when facing danger—like the time they faced Charoca, the angry rock monster.

Practical mind helps Naomi solve problems.

BEST FRIENDS

Although Naomi and Elena lead very different lives, they both love adventure, helping others, and having fun. Their different experiences and attitudes make them a perfect team.

Naomi in charge

Elena puts Naomi in charge of an archaeological dig. Elena knows that her best friend is ready to manage this important project.

High-flying friends

It takes Naomi a while to get used to flying on Migs, the jaquin—the ground is so far below! But she soon learns to love soaring with Elena.

Kind, caring heart helps Elena understand other people.

Teamwork

Sometimes, Elena and Naomi may not agree about the best way to solve a problem, but they always work things out in the end.

ESTEBAN

Chancellor Esteban is Elena's older cousin. He tries to appear wiser and more capable than Elena. However, what Esteban really wants deep down is his family's love and acceptance.

Out of control

Esteban's desire to control everything can lead to trouble—like the time he smashed a crystal wall and freed a mischievous creature called a duende.

Finger used for pointing the blame at others.

Wrong impression

Esteban tries to impress the visiting King Toshi of Satu by performing a Satu dance. Big mistake. King Toshi wants to learn about Avalor!

Youthful dreams

Esteban loves to remember the days of his youth. He wishes he could be young again.

"It will be clear... who is the real power behind the throne." Esteban

Carefully styled hair

Smart goatee and mustache

Always dressed to impress.

Personal Guard

Esteban has his own personal Royal Guard, named Higgins. Higgins is loyal, but he isn't as smart or daring as Elena's Guard, Gabe.

True or false?

Esteban is Elena's uncle.

False.
He is her much older cousin. While Elena was trapped in the amulet, Esteban continued to age.

Perfectionist

Proud Esteban wants to appear perfect, so he is quick to blame others when things go wrong. After all, he is royal. He doesn't make mistakes.

FAMILY FIRST

While Elena learns how to rule Avalor, she also makes sure to find time to care for her family. It's not always easy, but Elena knows that family comes first!

Love goes two ways

Elena has learned the importance of family from her grandparents. Luisa and Francisco always look out for Elena, and Elena wants to take care of them.

Happy birthday, Esteban!

Esteban thinks everyone has forgotten his birthday. Not true! Elena has planned a surprise party for him.

True or false?

Esteban was raised by Luisa and Francisco.

True. He is their grandson and they love him.

Close sisters

Their parents may be gone, but Elena and Isabel have each other. They know they can fully rely on one another.

The right choice

Esteban sacrifices his bottle of water from the Fountain of Youth in order to save Elena. She matters more to him than his chance to be young again.

Perfect gift

The journal Elena gives Isabel is more than just a book. It's a gift that shows how much Elena believes in her sister's abilities.

DAY OF THE DEAD

Day of the Dead (Dia de los Muertos) is one of Elena's favorite days of the year. It is a time to celebrate and remember the people she loves.

Best altar ever!

Elena decorates an altar display for her mother and father with marigolds, a tiara and crown, candles, and food they loved.

Fabulous food

It's fun to prepare special food, including colorful sugar skull cookies, candied pumpkin, and sweet bread —a favorite of Elena's mom.

Family memories

Remembering good times with her parents makes Elena happy. She knows they are still with her in her heart.

Cool costumes

At dusk everyone dresses in colorful costumes and heads to the cemetery with food, flowers, and candles. It's time to celebrate!

Naomi
Best friend

- *Understands people*
- *Knows what people want—and need*
- *Gives good advice and makes sure Elena listens to it!*
- *Never gives up and is very determined*
- *Makes Elena laugh*

Luisa
Loving abuela (grandmother)

- *Always stays calm*
- *Looks on the bright side*
- *Is positive and kind*
- *Is nice to everyone!*
- *Reminds Elena to believe in herself*

Many meetings

Most of the Grand Council meetings are serious, but sometimes they can be fun. The meetings give Elena and her advisors the chance to listen to the people of Avalor.

Francisco
Wonderful abuelo (grandfather)

- Is the wisest person Elena knows (even if he is a bit set in his ways)
- Is patient and thoughtful
- Has a song for everything!
- Reminds Elena to slow down and think

Esteban
Smart cousin

- Knows a lot about the kingdom and everyone in it
- Is an expert on proper royal behavior
- Is super organized
- Is a bit pushy, but tries to help Elena

GRAND COUNCIL

Elena is excited to have chosen her Grand Council. Each person she has picked is unique and special. With their help, Elena hopes to rule wisely and respectfully.

GABE

Handsome, headstrong Gabe takes his role as Elena's Royal Guard very seriously. He always has Elena's best interests at heart, even if he sometimes gets a bit carried away with defending the Princess!

Spirited steed
Gabe's speedy horse, Fuego, has a fiery temperament. Getting on Fuego isn't the hard part. Staying on is.

Have you heard?
Gabe's parents really want him to work at the family bakery.

Act first, think later
Sometimes Gabe draws conclusions—and his sword—too fast. He once fought a group of Noblins, who just wanted to go home.

"It's my job to protect you."
Gabe to Elena

Dashingly handsome

Loyal Guard

Gabe would follow Elena anywhere and do anything for her. She trusts him completely, and he becomes one of her best friends.

Blue and red uniform of Avalor Royal Guard

True or false?

Gabe has a secret crush on Elena.

True. He's felt that way since the first day they met.

Wizard versus Guard

Sometimes a sword is no match for magic—like the time the evil wizard Fiero turned Gabe into a stone statue.

Boots polished to a shine.

Friendly rivalry

Gabe and Mateo don't always see eye to eye. They both want to help Elena, but they often disagree on the best way to do so.

DANGER!

Elena goes on many exciting adventures. Some of them are full of danger, but the brave Princess is fast-thinking and daring. She is prepared to face any danger to protect her kingdom and the people she loves.

Captured!

When Noblins capture Isabel and Gabe, nothing can stop Elena from flying to the rescue. That's her sister after all!

Duende invasion

When mischievous duendes open a gateway that will allow thousands more duendes to invade Avalor, Naomi has great ideas to stop them. Like any great leader, Elena listens!

Quicksand rescue
On the magical island of Santalos, Esteban gets stuck in quicksand. It's up to Elena and Mateo to pull him to safety—but they must act fast.

River of fire
Red-hot lava is racing toward a village. But Elena stays calm and convinces Charoca, the angry rock creature, to cool the lava down in time.

Turned to stone
Elena must risk being turned to stone in order to defeat the evil wizard Fiero and free her grandparents from his spell.

CAN YOU KEEP AVALOR SAFE?

Avalor is a happy, beautiful place, but that doesn't mean it is always safe from danger. Can you help protect Avalor? Be careful, be brave, and good luck!

START

Are you strong enough to stand up to an evil moth fairy's powerful dark magic?

NO

YES

Sometimes things don't go to plan. Do you have the determination to keep trying when a task is difficult and you're tired?

NO

YES

Charoca is angry. When he gets angry, his volcano gets dangerous. Are you good at calming people down when they are upset?

NO

YES

Three duendes are on the loose! They are tricky and hard to catch. Are you good at solving problems?

NO

YES

Are you willing to face danger to protect the people you love?

NO

YES

Oops!
Then you might
as well go to
bed. It's going
to get dark
really soon.

Oh no!
The volcano is
getting hotter and
hotter. Avalor is
about to become
a city of fire.

Uh-oh!
The duendes
won. I hope the
people of Avalor
like little green
creatures.

**WELL
DONE!**
Avalor is safe
once more!

JAQUINS

Jaquins are half-bird, half-jaguar creatures who roam the skies of Avalor. Although they can be mischievous, they are extremely loyal and are always ready to help Elena and her friends.

Oops!

While playing, the jaquins accidentally break a statue in Avalor City. They discover it was guarding a secret, ancient chamber

Powerful, feathered macaw wings

Flying friendship

Elena loves riding on Skylar's back. He and his friends are like magical steeds of the sky.

Migs

Migs is sometimes grumpy—but that's because he is trying to keep his friends Skylar and Luna under control! Migs has traveled far and wide, and is very wise.

Powerful ally

When Elena needs help rescuing a Marposa who is stuck in some roots, Skylar uses his great strength to set the creature free.

Skylar

Skylar can be careless, but this fun-loving troublemaker is also incredibly loyal. He will do anything for Elena.

Unique coloring and coat pattern

Luna

Luna is a daredevil, always joking and usually causing trouble. She is pretty good at getting her cousin Skylar to join in as well.

True or false?

Jaquins come from the realm of Vallestrella.

True.
It is their homeland. It can be accessed from Avalor through a magical cave gateway.

Sleek jaguar body is agile and strong.

TRAVEL LIKE A PRINCESS

Crown Princess Elena travels throughout the kingdom to meet and help her subjects. Whether she is sailing, soaring, or galloping, she always rides in royal style.

True or false?
Skylar is always ready to give Elena a lift.

True.
All Elena has to do is call his name.

Royal Cruiser

There's nothing as relaxing as a day at sea, especially on an elegant ship like Elena's Royal Cruiser. It's the perfect way to take to the waves.

Covered viewing area

Beautiful Avaloran decoration

Flag of Avalor

Majestic jaquin

Elena loves flying on Skylar. The strong, powerful jaquin can carry her to hard-to-reach places fast. She adores the feeling of freedom she gets from flying.

Have you heard?

Elena's horse is named Canela, which means "cinnamon" in Spanish.

Speedy steed

Elena's beautiful, energetic horse is always ready for a wild and daring ride. Fast is good. Faster is even better!

Royal Coach

When Elena needs to make a special appearance in the city or travel with friends and family, her Royal Coach offers both comfort and regal style.

"It's not just about how many spells you know..."
Elena to Mateo

Disappearing island

No one can stay too long on the Island of Santalos. The magical island disappears at sundown, and so will anyone who is there at that time.

Light magic

Elena's Scepter of Light is an ancient Maruvian treasure that helps her channel the magic within herself. Elena is learning to master it.

Fountain of Youth

The magical water from the Fountain of Youth can make a person young again. However, too many sips can make a person far younger than they'd like!

Protective magic

There is both good and bad magic in Avalor. Luckily for Elena and her friends, Mateo's spells can protect them from harm.

MAGICAL KINGDOM

Avalor is full of magic. Usually, it is glorious and wonderful! However, in the wrong hands, it can be dangerous. Elena and her friends must learn to respect the magic they encounter on their adventures.

Powerful petals

A nibble of this magical flower can return a person to their true age. Mateo picks the flower to help Esteban, who has aged backward into a baby!

WANTED

Fiero

Dark wizard searching
for the Codex Maru,
an ancient spellbook.
Last seen entering the
Royal Palace, disguised
as a kindly old man.

Reward: A lifetime supply of the finest Avaloran chocolates.

Beware!

Fiero uses a black tamborita
(drum wand) to turn anyone
in his way into a stone statue.
He can only be defeated
by a powerful wizard.

Do not approach him.

Orizaba

Evil moth fairy intent on plunging Avalor into permanent darkness. Last seen heading to Sunstone with the Eye of Midnight.

WANTED

Reward: A private audience with Crown Princess Elena.

Caution!

Orizaba uses dangerous purple smoke that can blast through obstacles or stun people. She can only be defeated by a magical light from a powerful weapon.

Do not attempt capture.

Lessons Learned

It takes experience and practice to become a wise ruler. On her many adventures, Elena gets plenty of both! With each challenge she and her friends face, Elena learns lots of important lessons.

1. Listen and learn
When naughty Noblins steal a ship, Elena leaps into action. But when she hears their side of the story, she realizes the homesick creatures need her help!

2. Confidence counts!
Esteban accidently frees the duendes, but he won't listen to Naomi's ideas for capturing them. It's a good thing Naomi has faith in herself.

3. Be understanding
Charoca wants people to stop stealing his rocks. Only kind Elena tries to understand why this might make him angry, and respects his feelings.

What I've learned:

1. Look, listen, and learn. Find out what the situation really is before acting!

2. Trust yourself. Believe in your skills and what you know. But always be ready to learn more.

3. Show respect to others. Treating people kindly cools their anger.

4. Be patient. Learning new skills is hard and takes practice.

5. Be a team player. No one has all the right answers all the time.

4. Practice makes perfect
Elena needs to spend more time figuring how and why her magic Scepter works before she can use it safely.

5. Work together
Elena and her friends must learn to work as a team—even when it seems like there is no solution to their problem!

King Hector

King Hector thinks everyone should do what he wants. Can Elena challenge the bossy bully?

Doña Paloma

Powerful, strong-willed Doña Paloma is head of Avalor's Traders' Guild. She is very focused on making money.

King Toshi

Gracious, good-humored King Toshi from the kingdom of Satu believes that family comes first.

NEW FACES

Princess Elena meets with many important leaders and rulers from other kingdoms. Some of them are very different to Elena, but she must learn to get along with them all.

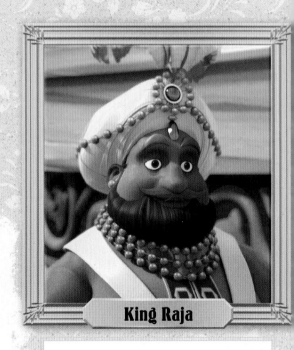

King Raja

King Raja of Napurna is a timid ruler. Elena wants to inspire him to stand up for himself and do what's right.

King Joaquin

King Joaquín of Cariza is a polite, soft-spoken ruler. He helps Elena deal with King Hector's bullying behavior.

Prince Alonso

Prince Alonso of Cordoba thinks he is charming. Actually, he is a spoiled prince who has no interest in ruling.

King Juan Ramón

This strong leader is frustrated by the behavior of his son, Prince Alonso. He admires Elena's passion for ruling.

King Lars

King Lars of Maarswik finds it hard to oppose the pushy King Hector. Elena helps him become a stronger leader.

Spirited helper

Elena must decide whether to help a grandmother ghost resolve an argument between her grandchildren. If she does, she risks missing her own family's Day of the Dead celebrations.

Stand up, stand out

On King Hector's royal island retreat, Elena tries to fit in—until a baby Marposa needs her help. Should Elena defy bossy King Hector and stand up for what's right?

DIFFICULT DECISIONS

Crown Princess Elena has many decisions to make. Sometimes it's hard to figure out what to do! But when Elena follows her heart, it usually leads to the right answer.

Keeping a promise

Elena is torn between welcoming important palace visitors and a promise she made to help Isabel. Elena must decide which comes first—her family or her royal duties.

WHAT TYPE OF LEADER ARE YOU?

Do you love coming up with fun ideas for family and friends? Do you enjoy helping them solve problems? Or do you just want them to do exactly what you say? Take this quiz to find out what kind of leader you are!

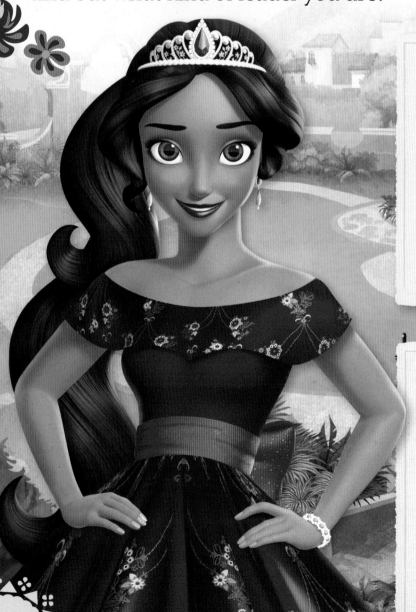

1

Your friend is upset. Do you...

A) Listen carefully and help her figure out a good solution.
B) Take charge. You can fix everything—you think.
C) Oops—too busy playing to help out. Maybe later.
D) Tell her to do exactly what you say.

2

When playing a sport, what role do you want to play?

A) One of the team. It's more fun!
B) The coach, so I can tell everyone what to do.
C) I prefer cheering from the sidelines.
D) I have to be the star player.

3

What do you want your friends to think about you?

A) That they can count on me.
B) That I'm really smart.
C) That I'm always ready for fun.
D) That I give great gifts.

4

If you had one magical power, what would it be?

A) The power to make people smile.
B) The power to make people admire me.
C) The power to make people quit bossing me around.
D) The power to make everyone do what I want.

5

If you make a silly mistake, do you...

A) Laugh about it and learn from it.
B) Tell everyone it wasn't a mistake at all.
C) Pretend it's someone else's fault.
D) Get angry at anyone who laughs at you.

Mostly As – Elena
Caring
You want what's best for everyone, and your friends know they can count on you. But you can get carried away sometimes. Slow down and think before you help!

Mostly Bs – Esteban
Controlling
You love taking control. But you need to listen to others more. When you do, your natural abilities to organize and plan will be your strengths.

Mostly Cs – Prince Alonso
Carefree
Having fun is great, and everyone loves how easy-going you are, but be careful your playful attitude doesn't turn into laziness. When you learn to do your share, you'll be amazing.

Mostly Ds – King Hector
Demanding
You tend to get angry when people don't agree with you. Let someone else be right once in a while. It's a teamwork thing.

ACKNOWLEDGMENTS

Project Editors Shari Last, Ruth Amos
Senior Designer Lynne Moulding
Designer Lisa Rogers
Pre-production Producer Kavita Varma
Producer Zara Markland
Managing Editor Sadie Smith
Managing Art Editor Ron Stobbart
Art Director Lisa Lanzarini
Publisher Julie Ferris
Publishing Director Simon Beecroft

First American Edition, 2017
Published in the United States by DK Publishing
345 Hudson Street, New York, New York 10014

Page design copyright © 2017 Dorling Kindersley Limited
DK, a Division of Penguin Random House LLC

17 18 19 20 21 10 9 8 7 6 5 4 3 2 1
001–297996–July/17

A catalog record for this book is available
from the Library of Congress.

ISBN: 978-1-4654-5554-3

DK books are available at special discounts when
purchased in bulk for sales promotions, premiums,
fund-raising, or educational use.
For details, contact: DK Publishing Special Markets,
345 Hudson Street, New York, New York 10014
SpecialSales@dk.com

Printed and bound in China

A WORLD OF IDEAS:
SEE ALL THERE IS TO KNOW

www.dk.com
www.disney.com